Hercules Beetle

by Grace Hansen

INCREDIBLE INSECTS

Abdo Kids Jumbo is an Imprint of Abdo Kids
abdobooks.com

abdobooks.com

Published by Abdo Kids, a division of ABDO, P.O. Box 398166, Minneapolis, Minnesota 55439.
Copyright © 2022 by Abdo Consulting Group, Inc. International copyrights reserved in all countries.
No part of this book may be reproduced in any form without written permission from the publisher.
Abdo Kids Jumbo™ is a trademark and logo of Abdo Kids.

Printed in the United States of America, North Mankato, Minnesota.

052021

092021

 THIS BOOK CONTAINS
RECYCLED MATERIALS

Photo Credits: Alamy, iStock, Minden Pictures, Science Source, Shutterstock

Production Contributors: Teddy Borth, Jennie Forsberg, Grace Hansen
Design Contributors: Candice Keimig, Victoria Bates

Library of Congress Control Number: 2020947655
Publisher's Cataloging-in-Publication Data

Names: Hansen, Grace, author.
Title: Hercules beetle / by Grace Hansen
Description: Minneapolis, Minnesota : Abdo Kids, 2022 | Series: Incredible insects | Includes online
        resources and index.
Identifiers: ISBN 9781098207380 (lib. bdg.) | ISBN 9781644945582 (pbk.) | ISBN 9781098208226
        (ebook) | ISBN 9781098208646 (Read-to-Me ebook)
Subjects: LCSH: Hercules beetle--Juvenile literature. | Rhinoceros beetle--Juvenile literature. | Beetles--
        Juvenile literature. | Insects--Juvenile literature. | Insects--Behavior--Juvenile literature.
Classification: DDC 595.7--dc23

Table of Contents

Hercules Beetles 4

Food 16

Life Cycle 18

More Facts 22

Glossary 23

Index 24

Abdo Kids Code. 24

Hercules Beetles

The Hercules beetle is the largest type of **rhinoceros beetle**. It is also one of the largest beetles in the world. It can grow up to 7 inches (17.8 cm) long!

Hercules beetles can be found in Central and South America. They live in tropical rainforests. The beetles **burrow** in piles of leaves, plants, and fallen logs.

The Hercules beetle got its name for its strength. It can lift 850 times its own weight. That would be like a human lifting an armored tank!

Females are often brownish-black in color. Males usually have a black head and a black, brown, or green body. They are covered in black spots.

male

female

11

Males also have large, horn-like **pincers**. The pincers can be 2 to 3 inches (5 to 7.6 cm) long! They are used to fight off other males and to dig.

Hercules beetles are huge, but they can fly! Like all beetles, they have tough **elytra** that cover and protect their wings. The elytra lift up so the soft inner wings can open for flight.

elytron ————

inner wing

Food

Hercules beetles spend their days hiding. At night, they come out to eat. They mainly feed on fruits and tree sap.

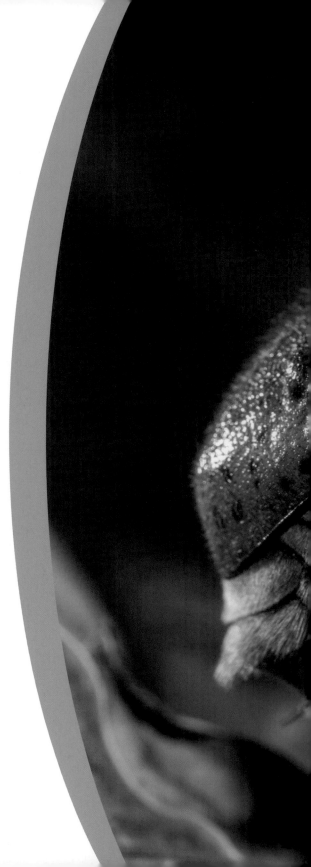

Life Cycle

Females lay around 100 eggs in rotting wood. **Larvae** hatch from these eggs. They can reach 2 inches (5 cm) in size!

egg

larval growth stages

Larvae mainly eat dead wood and plants. This helps keep rainforests healthy. After around 18 months, they will **pupate**. About 32 days later, adult Hercules beetles will appear!

Hercules beetle pupa

More Facts

- In Japan, large beetles are good luck charms. They are symbols of strength.

- A Hercules beetle's **pincers** can grow to be longer than its body!

- The entire life cycle of a Hercules beetle can last up to 2 years.

Glossary

burrow – to dig into.

elytra – the pair of hardened forewings of certain insects, like beetles, that form a protective covering for the flight wings.

larva – an insect after it hatches from an egg and before it changes into its adult form. A larva does not have any wings and looks like a worm.

pincer – one of a pair of grasping, jaw-like body parts on certain insects and animals that are used for griping things and fighting.

pupate – to become a pupa. A pupa is an insect in the middle stage of its development, after it is a larva. It does not eat or move. It is changing into its adult form.

rhinoceros beetle – any of the various large, mainly tropical beetles with horns.

Index

Central America 6

color 10

eggs 18

flight 14

food 16, 20

habitat 6

larvae 18, 20

markings 10

pincers 12

pupating 20

size 4, 12, 14, 18

South America 6

species 4

strength 8

wings 14

Abdo Kids
ONLINE
FREE! ONLINE MULTIMEDIA RESOURCES

Visit **abdokids.com**
to access crafts, games,
videos, and more!